D1370650

**THE
SECRET
OF A
SPIRIT-
FILLED
LIFE**

THE SECRET OF A SPIRIT-FILLED LIFE

CHARLES L. CHANEY

TYNDALE
House Publishers, Inc.
Wheaton, Illinois

Fifth printing, September 1985

Library of Congress Catalog Card Number
76-46111. ISBN 0-8423-5850-1, paper.
Copyright © 1973 by Charles L. Chaney.
Originally published under the title *Take,*
by Church Growth Books, Springfield,
Illinois. Reissued in 1976 by Tyndale
House Publishers, Wheaton, Illinois, by
permission of Church Growth Books and
the author. All rights reserved.

Printed in the United States of America.

To F. E. C.,
who alone knows
what I have been
and what I am.
Only she can verify
the assertion
in this booklet
that Christ continues
to make me new.

CONTENTS

Expose yourself to the light
Confess your sins to God
Accept the work of your advocate

The problem of Christian living
The path of Christian victory
The pattern of the Christian life

The invitation
To whom is the invitation addressed?
What does the invitation ask us to do?
What happens when we accept the
    invitation?

Who is the Holy Spirit?
When did the Holy Spirit begin his work?
Why was the Holy Spirit given?
What is the Holy Spirit's ministry in the
    life of a Christian?
How can you be filled with the Holy
    Spirit?
Keys to exercising faith

PREFACE

This booklet is a personal testimony. As such, it is only an *interim report*. It does not contain all the truth about "life at its best." It articulates some of my recent discoveries, which have made life in Jesus Christ a true adventure. These discoveries have enabled me to live, from my own perspective at least, on a higher plane. (If you wish to find out if I'm really different, you will have to ask my wife, my children, and my friends.)

I use the word *discoveries,* but that is only a manner of speaking. There is only one discovery: Jesus Christ. Christ is the secret plan of God for ultimate victory in the life of every Christian. The one and only discovery I have made is that Jesus has not only redeemed me from sin by his death, but he also saves me by his life.

The Christian life is in reality only the Christ life. Christ actually wants to live his own life new and fresh in me every day.

In addition to being a kind of personal testimony, this booklet is an outgrowth of reading the Bible with new eyes. At this point also, I do not speak *ex cathedra*. But I do say the Bible has been a new and living book over the past five years. Much that was obscure and insignificant is now thought-provoking and exhilarating. I pray God it shall continue to be so.

These chapters, as will be obvious, are problem-oriented. They are directed to four major areas where we average Christians seem to be most in trouble. I might have given them different titles. "How to know joy," "How to know victory," "How to have rest," and "How to be filled" describe the contents of each chapter. I have discussed these topics over and over again in recent months, and everywhere I find people hungry to know Christ at a deeper level. Thousands of people are disillusioned with bootstrap religion (trying to "do it" themselves by much prayer, many devotionals, much holy living). They always fail, and that will always be the case. What triumph there is, what relief when we loosen those straps and *take* what is already ours in Jesus Christ. Then prayer becomes a delight, Bible study a joy, and holy living a natural consequence. What we have becomes, in the process, something highly contagious. Wherever we go, almost without trying, we kindle little fires of God in the souls of others.

CHAPTER ONE

TAKE OFF THE MASK

The first principle of a full and meaningful life is honesty. We must be honest about what we are and what we do. There is no shortcut. We can never experience the quality of life that is the heritage of the child of God until we come out from behind the masks of respectability, self-righteousness, and pseudopiety that hide our real selves. After living behind these veneers, we convince ourselves that we have everything God purposed for this life. At the same time, we wonder why we so easily fall into our own private sins, why we are often so miserable, and why we have no vital, everyday contact with God.

Many of us Christians live defeated lives, almost totally devoid of joy, based on something God did in us years ago. Our present life is not grounded on what God is doing in and for us in the *eternal present*. We experience little victory or communion with God. We have nothing within us to share. We spend all our strength preserving a memory rather than sharing the excitement of *right now*.

Three important questions are asked constantly by modern Christians: When I sin, how can I be cleansed, since I am already a Christian? How can I know joy, even in times of trouble? How can I have direct fellowship with God every day?

All three problems are correctly solved by the same answer. Just as the sums of two plus four, three plus three, and five plus one are all six, the answer to each of these three questions is identical. It is found in 1 John 1:5—2:2. This paragraph gives three principles of daily living that will enable you to come to purity, joy, and continuous fellowship with the Father, Son, and your brothers and sisters.

Expose yourself
to the light

First, if you would experience life at its best, you must expose yourself to the "light."

> This is the message God has given to us to pass on to you: that God is Light and in him is no darkness at all. So if we say we are his friends, but go on living in spiritual darkness and sin, we are lying. But if we are living in the light of God's presence, just as Christ does, then we have wonderful fellowship and joy with each other, and the blood of Jesus his Son cleanses us from every sin (1 John 1:5-7, TLB).

We seldom want to come to the light, but we enjoy hearing truth about someone else. In fact, we insist with a passion that the full truth be known about everything, just so it doesn't adversely affect us or our family. We are very slow to let God, who is light, really shine in our lives and expose the flaws in our own character and conduct.

However, the answer to the biblical question, "How shall a young man cleanse his way?" is that the individual (young or old, male or female) expose himself to the light of God, moment by moment. Walk in the light! Then the blood of Jesus Christ cleanses us from our sins.

What does this mean? Blood is, among other things, the cleansing agent of the body. One of my friends developed active tuberculosis a few years ago. She was immediately placed in a sanitarium in suburban Chicago. Her physician explained that her disease usually infects people who have never learned to relax, even in sleep. The long bedrest required for healing gives the blood opportunity to do its total cleansing work. It is the blood that washes away the infection and impurities in the lungs. Just so, as we expose ourselves to God's light, the blood of Christ cleanses us from all sin.

The reason for coming to the light is obvious. Light reveals things as they are. My parents operated a small town grocery store in central Texas. We purchased eggs from the people of the surrounding area. The eggs were put in crates and trucked each week to Fort Worth where they were boxed and sold by the dozen. In the summer, since most of the eggs were fertile, we had to be very careful. If the eggs were kept too long before taking them to market, they would be either rotten or beginning to form into chicks. So through each hot season, we would "candle" all the eggs we purchased. We cut a small hole in a little wooden box and put a light bulb inside. When we held an egg up to the hole, the light would shine through its shell. We could see if the yolk was broken or spotted. The true condition of the egg was discovered by exposing it to light.

A recent report on the manufacture of cultured pearls explained that there is only one way to distinguish a fine cultured stone from a true natural one. Only an X-ray can reveal the heart of the pearl. A natural gem is formed around an irregular particle. A cultured stone forms around a perfect bead placed in the oyster by man. A powerful light reveals the true nature of the pearl.

Only the light can show the truth about ourselves. To live the cleansed life, we must expose ourselves to the light of God.

How does one expose himself to the light? Here is one way to begin. Take a sheet of paper and number down the side. Write on that piece of paper everything in your life that is displeasing to God. Be perfectly honest. Don't show the list to anyone. You don't have to hide a single thing. Write down everything.

When finished, pray this prayer: "Lord, you are light. Shine in me and show me anything else in my life that is displeasing to you." If you are completely honest, God will show you many things. Your list will be long.

When you have done this, move on to the second principle.

Confess your sins to God

If we say that we have no sin, we are only fooling ourselves, and refusing to accept the truth. But if we confess our sins to him, he can be depended on to forgive us and to cleanse us from every wrong. (And it is perfectly proper for God to do this for us because Christ died to wash away our sins.) If we claim we have not sinned, we are lying and calling God a liar, for he says we have sinned (1 John 1:8-10, TLB).

Confession is the beginning of honesty. A person cannot be honest about other things or other people until he is first honest about himself.

Confession is the end of pretense. You no longer have to wear a mask. You can relax. You don't have to maintain a front. Don't continue the farce.

Confession is the indispensable ingredient of transparency, of being completely pure of heart. It is the pure of heart, those who have expelled the devious and hypocritical, who see God.

Confession is the absolute prerequisite for fellowship with God. God already knows the truth about you. You can never hide what you are and do, or wish to do, from God.

Unconfessed sin always clogs the channels of joy. There is no way joy can flow until we are honest with God. What release, what cleansing there is in confession.

"No," you object, "that's too easy. If forgiveness is that easy, I'm really going to swing. I'll sin all I want to and live it up. Then I'll ask forgiveness and go my way again."

First, if you say that this is too easy, you imply that there is something you must do to earn or deserve God's forgiveness. You suggest that there is something you must suffer to get God to forgive your sin. There is no suffering you can undergo, no price you can pay, no penalty you can endure that will obligate God to forgive you. Christ has already paid the full price. There is no additional cost you can meet. The only reason God will forgive you is that he loves you and Christ has suffered for you. Forgiveness is not easy. It cost the death of God's Son. Don't presume that you can, by suffering or service, earn what God will only give you freely by his grace.

Second, if you have an attitude that jumps to take advantage of God's grace in forgiveness, then I warn you that you are not exhibiting the spirit of Christ. If you do not have the spirit of Christ, you are not his. You see, the Christian's problem is not that he is forbidden to sin as much as he wants. The Christian's problem is that he sins more than he wants. He wishes he didn't sin as much as he does.

And how can we be sure that we belong to him? By looking within ourselves: are we really trying to do what he wants us to? Someone may say, "I am a Christian; I am on my way to heaven; I belong to Christ." But if he doesn't do what Christ tells him to, he is a liar (1 John 2:3, 4, TLB).

What the true Christian wants to know is, "When I sin, how do I restore a right relationship to the Father?" The answer is, "If we confess our sins, he ... will [freely and fully] forgive our sins and cleanse us from all unrighteousness" (1 John 1:9).

But you may say, "Won't God get tired of my coming? I repeat the same sins and have to ask forgiveness so often that God will get fed up with me if I come back again and again. When he has forgiven me once, and I learn my lesson, he surely won't maintain the same attitude toward me."

Let me assure you that although you try to do his will, you will never do it perfectly. As you try to walk in your own strength and do God's will, you are bound to fail. You will discover what Paul learned a long time ago. "When I want to do good, I don't; and when I try not to do wrong, I do it anyway" (Rom. 7:19, TLB).

God is already fed up with you. He knows you are going to fail. He knows what you are and what you will do when left to yourself.

Left to myself, I always fail. I can take something that is good, helpful, and holy, and, in a flash, I can think of a way to get glory for myself out of it. I am subject to lying about anything, if God doesn't speak truth in me. I will inevitably act selfishly, left to myself.

In our own strength we can do nothing but fail. God wants us finally to give up in despair and let him begin his will in us. I was talking about this in Oklahoma. A lady came to me and said, "I don't agree with you. You're telling me that I'm bound to fail. If I know I'm going to fail, I just want to quit. Is that really what you're saying?"

I said, "Yes, that's what I'm saying. But I'm really only repeating what Jesus said in John 15, 'Without me you can do nothing,' and what Paul said in Romans 7, 'I know that no good thing dwells in me.' I'm just repeating what they said. If you're ready to quit and agree that you can do nothing alone, you're near the place where Christ can begin to live his life in your body."

What commandment of God have you ever kept? Not one. You cannot keep them. Only Christ can keep them. If you kept one, you would be so proud that your pride would be sinful. Only Christ can live the obedient life in you.

Again, the second principle of a life of joy is "Confess your sins to God." "Confess" literally means "to agree with." Therefore, when you confess your sins, it means you agree with God about what you are and what you do. He sees your sin as evil, contemptible, and something you should turn from, and you see it the same way. Confession therefore involves a change of attitude toward what you do, and it concerns what you are in truth. It involves a "willingness to be willing" to let go of whatever in your life is displeasing to God.

How shall you begin? Take the list you made and one by one confess those things that are displeasing to God. Lay them over on Jesus, who died for them. Then go on to the third principle.

Accept the work of your advocate

This principle is also essential. Accept by faith the work of your advocate in heaven, Jesus Christ.

> My little children, I am telling you this so that you will stay away from sin. But if you sin, there is someone to plead for you before the Father. His name is Jesus Christ, the one who is

all that is good and who pleases God
completely. He is the one who took
God's wrath against our sins upon
himself, and brought us into
fellowship with God; and he is the
forgiveness for our sins, and not only
ours but all the world's (1 John 2:1, 2,
TLB).

One of the greatest barriers to the cleansed
life of joy and fellowship with God is our
ingrained unwillingness to accept the work
of our advocate and with thanksgiving step
out as persons who are free and forgiven.

Let me say one thing. Restitution may
first have to be made. Some of your sins may
be against others. Apologies may need to
be made, things stolen may need to be paid
for or returned, words that did damage
may need to be withdrawn. Such things
govern whether you can accept full
forgiveness.

Some people don't accept the work of
Jesus because they fear some hidden sin
they may not have confessed. Don't be
super-introspective. Confess those sins that
God brings to your mind. If you did
something you don't remember, God will
call it to your attention in his good time.

Others don't accept the work of Jesus because they don't "feel" forgiven. You can't live the Christian life victoriously by "feeling" or by the evidence of outward circumstances. The Christian life must be lived on the basis of faith in the facts of God. When you confess your sin, he freely forgives, no matter how you feel. Your forgiveness does not depend on how you feel. It depends on his unalterable promise. When you confess your sins, making restitution where necessary, you can boldly step out into joyous fellowship with God.

Without fail, if you will follow the technique I have described, you can have joy in your soul, have direct fellowship with God, and be cleaner than you have been since you were saved.

Let me tell you how to maintain this joy. Learn the technique called "spiritual breathing." Many Christians today are like spiritual asthmatics. They are filled with congestion and breathe only little breaths. We let our sins go unconfessed until they stack up in our souls, clogging all the air passages of our inner being. Spiritual breathing is as essential to a full and meaningful life as human breathing is to physical life. Whenever you sin, confess it at once. Breathe it out. Then breathe back in God's forgiveness and peace.

It works. Let me illustrate. Some time ago, I made an appointment with a printer. I thought it was for 1:00 p.m. At 1:30, when the printer hadn't arrived, I called his office and spoke very sharply to his secretary. I immediately knew that I had mistreated her, but I said nothing. She called back later and told me her boss had the appointment marked on his calendar for 2:00 p.m. I still said nothing. But I did ask the Lord's forgiveness and I knew I would need to apologize to those I had mistreated. A little later the printer arrived. He hadn't even been to his office. I told him that I had been angry, that I wanted to apologize to him, and that I would call his secretary and apologize to her. I called a couple of days later. When I told her who I was she said, "Yes, I should have recognized *your* voice."

I said, "I need to apologize to you. I spoke sharply to you the other day, and I was completely at fault. Will you please forgive me?" My, how she changed! That made all the difference in the world. Besides that, the pure joy of Christ came flooding back into my soul.

The best illustration, however,

happened in a church where I served for ten years. In a chilly Chicago spring, our furnace went out on a Sunday night. The last thing the chairman of the trustees said as we left the church was, "Pastor, I must leave town early in the morning. Could you call the heating company?" Monday morning came bright and warm. I forgot all about the furnace.

By Wednesday, however, the weather had turned cold again. When I arrived at the church I found the people shivering in their coats. "I sure hope those furnace repairmen get here tomorrow," I said. I was stating the truth. I did hope the furnace would be repaired on Thursday. But, in fact, I lied. I was trying to give the impression that I had called the heating company and that it was really not my fault the building was cold. I was the pastor. I had come to pray. Yet in less than two minutes I had told a lie.

Then the minister of music said, "Pastor, what's the word about the new pews for the choir? Will they be straight, or curved as I recommended?" I don't remember to this day the words I said, but the impression I gave was that the church furniture company had advised against curved pews.

The truth was that the pastor and trustees had decided they would be straight. In less than five minutes I had told two lies. The Lord was convicting me with waves of inner misery.

I knew I had to set things straight. So after we had sung a hymn, I rose and said, "I must make two things clear. This building is cold because I forgot to call the furnace man. And, Orville, the decision to have straight pews was made by the pastor and the trustees. I gave you a false impression."

There was no reason for me to lie to begin with. But when I confessed my sin, the peace of God came rushing back into my soul. The same will be true for you when you expose yourself to the light, confess your sins to God, and accept the work of your advocate Jesus Christ.

CHAPTER TWO

TAKE UP THE CROSS

For life to be full and meaningful, some things must be reviewed every day. They might be called the compass points of the Christian life. We take our directions from them. Every day we mark them and live in the light of their location in our lives. The first compass point, as we saw in chapter 1, is honesty about what we do.

The second compass point is identification with the death and resurrection of Christ. From one point of view it concerns an aspect of the atonement of Christ. From another it concerns the place of faith in the life of the Christian. From a third viewpoint we talk about the reality of the resurrection of Christ and its effects on the Christian's life.

Focus your attention on Luke 9:23: "He said to all, 'If any man would come after me, let him deny himself and take up his cross daily and follow me.' "

Jesus is not talking here about how to become a Christian or how to begin the Christian life (conversion). Rather he is describing the Christian life in its totality (discipleship). Instead of describing a segment, he defines the whole. The essentials of the Christian life are his theme. True discipleship involves denying self, taking up your cross daily, and following Christ.

This verse, therefore, deals with the Christian life at its depth. When we become disciples, with all that term implies, we will have broken down the barriers that keep us from life at its best. These words of Jesus point to the one great problem of Christian living—the self. They focus on the path of Christian victory—the cross. They mark the pattern of Christian life—Christ himself.

The problem of Christian living

When Jesus said, "Deny your*self*," he got right to the basic problem of Christian living—the ego, the self, old Number One. Denying self is something entirely different from denying one's self *things*. Some of us ridicule Christians who have gone in for "self-denial," those who have thought that you can deny yourself by giving up meat, drink, pleasure, or sleep for a certain period of time. Yet we too have developed a sort of evangelical, Protestant, pietistic asceticism. We wouldn't think of denying ourselves sweets or meats. We don't drink; we don't smoke; we don't curse, go to bad movies, dance, or a lot of other things. Not doing these things—denying these things to self—has become the measure of dedication and the essence of Christian living. "Old Joe," we say, "is a real consecrated Christian" (or dedicated or separated, depending on our locale). "He doesn't dance, smoke, drink, curse, tell smutty yarns, attend cocktail parties, or mow his lawn on Sunday." And thus what we don't do is how we earn our Christian reputation.

A decade ago, when I was a new resident of greater Chicago, a precinct captain came to my home, soliciting my vote. I inquired about her relationship to Christ. In the conversation she discovered I was a Baptist. "I know all about Baptists," she exclaimed. "How interesting," I said. "Tell me about them." "Well," she replied, "they don't believe in selling liquor by the drink." It's wonderful that Baptists have such a reputation for sobriety and temperance, but it's tragic that all she knew about Baptists was something they stood against. The Christian life doesn't consist in the abundance of things that we don't do.

I don't advocate that we take up smoking or get off the wagon. I'm saying that our basic problem is not what we do, but what we are. The truth is that when I don't smoke, drink, or curse, I haven't denied myself anything. I never did most of those things. If I had, that still wouldn't solve my problem. My problem is not my sins but my self. My sins are crucial. I thank God that Christ died for my sins; I can have forgiveness and peace with God. I rejoice and rest in that forgiveness and peace. But my sins continue. The more I struggle with them the more I am aware that I need radical treatment. My ultimate problem is not the things that I do or don't do, but rather what I am.

What shall I do with me? This is the "I" that must be denied. My self is the source of my sins. When the spring is poisonous, the entire stream is corrupt. Because of my own inner evil, even the good things I do are tainted.

Three Greek words are translated "deny" in the New Testament. One means "to speak against" and a second, "to disown." The third word translated "deny" (here, and in all the Gospel parallels to this verse) means "to deny utterly." It means to deny the claims of, the assertions of, the dominion of the self.

Many times I have walked down the corridors of my heart to the throne room in order to put myself to death, to deny my self utterly. Such an effort always ends like a nightmare. Just before I roll off the cliff, just before the terrible thing happens to me, I wake up. I can go so far in putting my self to death, but just before I do that terrible thing, I fail. I cannot deny my self. I will not deny my self. In spite of all my efforts and prayers, I live on. I will not put my self to death. And yet this is what must be done.

Charles Chaney will not be reformed. I don't need mouth-to-mouth resuscitation. I need a heart-to-heart resurrection. I must die and a new man must be born. No preventive or curative will suffice. I must have a new life.

The path of Christian victory

This brings me to the second phrase, "take up your cross daily." It is obvious that Jesus isn't here speaking of a literal, rough, wooden cross. He isn't calling for us to shoulder such an object each day and carry it around. That wouldn't get us anything but tired.

This is a metaphorical use of the word *cross*. There are a number of places in the Gospels where the word is used in this way (Matt. 10:38; 16:24; Mark 8:34; 10:21; Luke 9:23; 14:27). All have to do with discipleship at its depth. The metaphor explains how we must deal with the self.

"Bearing our cross" is a widely used expression. It is the pious way of speaking of certain burdens or situations that are unpleasant and troublesome. Our "cross," it can be said categorically, is not an oversexed husband, a neurotic wife, a thoughtless employer, chronic constipation, or a spastic child. It is not any other *thing*. "Cross" is a metaphor for death. This is the imagery of the word in the New Testament. For Jesus to bear his cross meant for him to die. For us to bear our cross must mean the same.

How shall I deliver my self to death? Which cross is *my* cross?

The answer to the first question is obvious: taking up my cross. Yet Watchman Nee astutely observes that it is impossible to commit suicide by crucifixion. There are many ways for a person to take his own life, but crucifixion is not one of them. Someone else must put that person to death on the cross. There is a true analogy in the metaphor. You cannot crucify yourself spiritually. You will not. Try as you will, you just won't drive in the nails.

Now to the second question. What is my cross? A vital part of the Good News of Jesus Christ is that my cross is identical with his cross. This aspect of the atonement is generally neglected or overlooked. I read the Bible for years and didn't see this truth about Christ's atoning death. Christ died *for* our sins. Because of his death for our sins we can stand just and righteous and at peace before God. But we also died *with* him on the cross. "We know that our old self was crucified with him so that the sinful body might be destroyed, and we might no longer be enslaved to sin" (Rom. 6:6). "I have been crucified with Christ; it is no longer I who live, but Christ who lives in me" (Gal. 2:20). "But far be it from me to glory except in the cross of our Lord Jesus Christ, by which the world has been crucified to me, and I to the world" (Gal. 6:14). "If with Christ you died to the elemental spirits of the universe, why do you live as if you still belonged to the world?" (Col. 2:20). For awhile another verse gave me some trouble: "And those who belong to Christ Jesus have crucified the flesh with its passions and desires" (Gal. 5:24). But I have studied that verse in its context, and it is only a way of speaking. For the crucifixion of "the flesh with its passions and desires" is part and parcel of my crucifixion with Jesus Christ.

Because Christ died for my sins I don't have to take the punishment I deserve for my sins. He suffered for me. By trusting him, forgiveness is mine. Christ's death is sufficient. There is no more price to pay for my sin. Even so, because I was with Christ on his cross, since I "have been united with him in a death like his" (Rom. 6:5), I also don't have to worry or struggle to put myself to death. I have been crucified with Christ.

As surely as he bore my sins he also bore my self on the cross. I am already dead with Christ, identified with him in his death. I was there when they crucified my Lord. I was crucified myself. The divine fact is: *I* am dead; I *am* dead; I am *dead!* Charles Chaney is no more. In truth, he died 2,000 years ago with Christ. What a relief. But that is only part of the story. I am not only dead. I am also buried "with Christ by baptism unto death."

And finally, the best news of all: I am raised with Christ from the dead that I may live unto God.

So, what is the path of victory: It is not to crucify yourself every day! It is to "take up your cross every day." To choose death to self, and, in the light of the eternal truth that you died with Christ, to yield your body to Christ. To allow him to live his life in you. To yield your members to him as instruments of righteousness. To permit him to incarnate himself in your body, so that he is your life (Col. 3:4).

I was amazed to discover 2 Corinthians 4:7-12. Among other things it says: "Are we always carrying in the body the death of Jesus, so that the life of Jesus may also be manifested in our bodies? For while we live we are always being given up to death for Jesus' sake, so that the life of Jesus may be manifested in our mortal flesh." Taking up your cross daily means always being given up to death for Jesus' sake. It means that we count (or reckon) ourselves "dead to sin and alive to God in Christ Jesus" (Rom. 6:11).

We accept the facts of our death and resurrection with Christ by *faith* just as we accept forgiveness in Christ by faith. That is what *to count* really means. An analogy can be found in the use of the sextant. Out on the high seas a sailor takes a sextant and focuses it on two fixed points: the horizon and a certain star. Then he calculates the ship's position and proceeds accordingly. That is called "reckoning." Our two points are our death with Christ and our resurrection with Christ. We focus on these two things:

(1) The old self is dead with Christ so that the sinful body can be destroyed and we

need no longer be enslaved to sin.

(2) We are raised with Christ from the dead so we can walk in newness of life.

Knowing these two things, we can yield ourselves to God as men and women alive from the dead.

The pattern of Christian life

This brings me to the third phrase, "and follow me." Every phrase in the New Testament that refers to our death with Christ also refers to our resurrection with him. The two are never separated. All the Bible quotations I included above show this. It is impossible to talk about "taking up your cross" without saying a great deal about what "and follow me" means.

However, I would like to make a distinction in emphasis by saying that in the cross we discover the path to victory and in Christ we find the pattern of Christian living. In fact, *Christ* is both the path of victory and the pattern of living. But the point I want to make is that it is a replication of his life—not in literal detail, but in quality and character—that Jesus intended. That was in fact the goal of the Father from the beginning. "We know that in everything God works for good with those who love him, who are called according to his purpose. For those whom he foreknew he also predestined to be conformed to the image of his Son, in order that he might be the first-born among many brethren" (Rom. 8:28, 29).

Did Jesus mean by *discipleship* literally to follow him from village to countryside to city? Had a man fulfilled the requirement of Jesus when he had actually done that?

Jesus didn't mean walking in his exact footsteps. Judas "followed" Jesus up and down the land of Judea and Galilee, but he did not, in fact, *follow* Jesus. When Jesus said "follow me" to his first disciples, he was talking about their becoming the kind of person he was. He was talking about the quality and character of their lives. His own life was to be the pattern. To follow means to become like him.

That this is one of the most important sayings of Jesus cannot be denied. What did these words mean to the early church? What should they mean to us?

"Follow me" means to follow the teaching of Jesus—to obey him, to do what

he has commanded. One who follows
Christ is one who obeys Christ. To follow
Christ is to "love your enemies," to
entertain not even the glance of lust, to
break not one jot or tittle of the law.

But I cannot love even my friends! If I
haven't committed the act of adultery, I
have been guilty with my eyes. I cannot and
do not keep the law. To will is present with
me, but how to perform it, I don't know. If
obedience through my own will, and in my
own strength, is what Jesus meant by "follow
me," I can never do it. I will never do it.

I think that obedience is only secondary to
what Jesus meant by "follow me." To the
early church the idea must have been closely
related to Paul's testimony: "I have been
crucified with Christ: and I myself no longer
live, but Christ lives in me." Acceptance of
the resurrection life is first, not obedience.
Not a slavish imitation, but a sort of
incarnation-yielding of our members as
instruments of righteousness (Rom. 6:13),
allowing Christ to fulfill his ministry in our
bodies, "that the life of Jesus may be
manifested in our mortal flesh" (2 Cor. 4:11).

Only Christ can be obedient. Only
Christ came to fulfill the law. We cannot do
it. But, thanks to God, that is what he

wants to do in us. He is our *life*. The Christian
life, as others have said much better than I,
is not nearly so much a changed life as an
exchanged life. Our life *is* actually changed.
It takes on a different quality because it has
been exchanged for the life of Christ.

The secret is to cease striving to
persevere. Rather, *present* yourself to God
as a person alive from the dead and *permit*
Christ to live in you. His life of obedience
is the pattern for your life as a Christian.
But, better than that, his life is also the
substance of it.

What have I learned? Every day I return
to these two divine facts: Charles Chaney
was crucified with Christ—I am a dead
man; and Charles Chaney is alive with him
forever more—or, what is much better,
Christ lives in me. Daily I review these
truths and invite the Holy Spirit to fill my
life. He makes the divine facts
flesh-and-blood reality in my life.

I say with Paul:

> But whatever gain I had, I counted as
> loss because of the surpassing worth of
> knowing Christ Jesus as Lord. For his
> sake I have suffered the loss of all
> things, and count them as refuse, in

order that I may gain Christ and be found in him, not having a righteousness of my own, based on law, but that which is through faith in Christ, the righteousness from God that depends on faith; that I may know him and the power of his resurrection, and may share his sufferings, becoming like him in his death, that if possible I may attain the resurrection from the dead. Not that I have already obtained this or am already perfect; but I press on to make it my own, because Christ Jesus has made me his own. Brethren, I do not consider that I have made it my own; but one thing I do, forgetting what lies behind and straining forward to what lies ahead, I press on toward the goal for the prize of the upward call of God in Christ Jesus (Philippians 3:7-14).

The first essential for a meaningful life is to be honest about what I do. I must deal with my sins. But I must also deal with myself. Only death will deliver me from self's dominion, but the truth is that I am already dead. My old self was with Christ on the cross. The way to win the victory over self is clear. Neither self-discipline nor self-inflicted punishment will suffice. We appropriate death to self by faith. "The righteous man lives by his faith" (Rom. 1:17).

CHAPTER THREE

TAKE ON THE YOKE

The believer faces several problems as he tries to live the Christian life. How do you maintain the thrill and happiness that often comes in the first flush of new life in Christ? It is almost universal for Christians to slip back into old patterns, fall back into past habits, and so find themselves in the same depressing routine they were in before they came to Christ.

What is the secret of joy? The secret, after your sins are confessed and forgiven right up to the moment, is to continue instant confession and immediate appropriation of the forgiveness and peace of God. It is what some Christians call spiritual breathing, learning to breathe out your sins immediately and breathe in God's mercy and forgiveness.

A second problem we wrestle with is self. We can reform what we *do,* but we don't have power to alter what we *are.* We will be selfish, we will be gluttonous, we will be envious. We will even take what we do in the name of Jesus and, in an instant, claim the glory for ourselves. How do you deal with self? The only solution to the self-problem is death. As in everything else, the Christian takes death to self by faith. Our old self was crucified with Christ. We accept the truth as the finished work of Christ and reckon ourselves dead indeed to sin but alive unto God. Daily reckoning of ourselves as dead, buried, but now risen with Christ's new life is the secret of victory over self.

A third problem the Christian faces is related to how we work for Christ. As new Christians we are so thankful for finding forgiveness that we want to go out and turn the world upside down for Jesus Christ. We roll up our sleeves and go to work. To our amazement, the world doesn't budge. We push and shove. We strain and jerk. We're astonished that others don't see things as we do. We're bewildered that all people don't come to the truth.

The invitation

While I was a pastor in Kentucky, a very aggressive young man was converted. He had been an outstanding baseball player in the area and was quite a fighter. He immediately started witnessing. To his dismay, his friends paid little attention to him. One night, standing outside the church building, he said, "I don't understand those guys, preacher. They don't pay attention to a thing I say."

Another friend, recently converted, was telling me about one of the fellows to whom he was witnessing. He said very seriously, "I think what he needs is for me to take him out and give him a good whipping."

We don't always say it that way, but we get just as frustrated. We can't understand why things don't go the way we want them to. We work hard, we do our best, we use our talents, but the walls don't come tumbling down.

51

We end up exhausted and despondent. If you think about it, you'll see that it really can't be any other way. If we succeeded by dint of our strength, we would be so proud and bigheaded that we would insist that the major glory belonged to us, not to God. We would let everybody know that at great sacrifice and effort we had really done something great for God. We would become, in our own eyes, God's indispensable servants.

Most of us suffer from what I choose to call an Abramic complex. Go back to that time in Abram's life when he and his wife were in despair because they had no children, though God had promised them an heir. Time was running out. Sarai came up with a brilliant suggestion. Abram could take that Egyptian girl, Hagar. The child she would bear would be considered Sarai's. Abram liked the idea. Not only did it please his fancy, but it had a religious dimension. He would be helping God fulfill his promise. We are never so eloquent as when we attempt to convince ourselves to do something morally questionable, but at the same time appealing to our own appetites. Abram and Hagar had a son named Ishmael. He was a wild man.

That's the kind of success I often have in God's work. Like Abram, I can't wait for God's promised child. I can't wait for God's time. I go in my own strength to help God do his work. Every time I do, the result is an Ishmael. Something comes to birth, but it's never what God intended. It's never the promised child.

The invitation of Jesus in Matthew 11:28-30 speaks specifically to this problem. It gives the secret of rest. "Come to me, all who labor and are heavy laden, and I will give you rest. Take my yoke upon you, and learn from me; for I am gentle and lowly in heart, and you will find rest for your souls. For my yoke is easy, and my burden is light."

Let's look at this invitation in detail.

To whom is the invitation addressed?

The invitation is addressed to the exhausted. That's the literal meaning of the word translated "all who labor." Everywhere I go, I find good, dedicated, hard-working Christians doing their best. But they accomplish very little, and they are worn to a frazzle. They go night and day doing their own work and that of the Lord. Contrary to what they have heard, the yoke is heavy.

In her book *Go Home and Tell*, Bertha Smith tells how, when she got to North China in 1918, she found a group of totally dedicated missionaries. They were called "the devotees" by other missionaries. They worked, prayed, and gave to the nth degree. But all they did was to dedicate their talents and gifts of the flesh to God's work. They attempted to do God's work for him in their own strength. They were exhausted and ineffective. This invitation is addressed to all men and women like them.

The invitation of Jesus is directed to all of us who have discovered the truth that the spirit is willing but the flesh is weak. It is addressed to those who are burdened with many duties, the heavy laden.

To many, the Christian life is an unending procession of duties. We do what we do, we live the way we live, because it is our Christian duty. The Christian life is based on "ought to" rather than "want to." We find ourselves crushed under the burden of duty, hobbled with unbreakable chains of obligation, laden with responsibilities. We never know the joy of *freedom.*

To live that way is to fall from the way of grace (Gal. 5:4). We don't lose our standing with God, but we regress to life under the law. We come again into bondage. The Christian life is freedom and joy and victory. It is living above the law because we do better than the law requires. When the Christian finds himself burdened with duties, Christ's invitation is addressed to him.

What does the invitation ask us to do?

1. Jesus invites us to come to him. One of the barriers we face in seeking rest is a tendency to look everywhere before we turn to Christ. We often unconsciously hold a "work philosophy" of the Christian life. We act as if Jesus has said, "Here is what I want you to do: love your enemy, love your neighbor, be perfect, always be happy, be holy, and be completely unselfish." Then, we surmise, he turns us loose. "Here is the way," Jesus says. "It's hard, it's impossible, but I've shown you the way. If you can do

it, I'll give you a pat on the back and let you into heaven."

Consequently, we turn everywhere for relief. We devise all kinds of plans, engage in all types of programs, and study the wisdom of the ages. We turn to everyone but Christ. Consciously or unconsciously, he has become our problem, not our problem-solver. He got us into this mess.

Christ hasn't left us alone to do our best to meet impossible demands. In fact, he doesn't want us merely to do our best for him; he knows how inadequate our best is. He wants to do his best in us. "Christ in you" is the hope of glory. To find rest, we must turn to him.

2. Jesus invites us to take on his yoke. What does this mean? Some scholars say it means we make Christ our mentor. Students always classify teachers. When our youngest son was going into third grade, he came home despondent. He had been told he was going to be in Mrs. Ortman's class the following year. She was the "meanest" teacher in that school. He had discovered that he would have to wear Mrs. Ortman's yoke for a year. Scholars suggest that this phrase, "take my yoke upon you," is an expression of the teacher-student

relationship. A young rabbi might say, "I've taken on the yoke of old Gamaliel. He is my teacher." Jesus invites us to become his students.

Others ask what a carpenter did in first-century Galilee. He certainly didn't build split-levels, ranch houses, and Cape Cods. Houses were made of mud and stone. A carpenter in the first century was a maker of yokes and furniture. Jesus, then, was a yoke maker. A carefully fashioned yoke may have hung over the carpenter shop in Nazareth. Yoke making was a rather long process. The oxen were brought back again and again to have the yoke fitted just right. Jesus may have been using this experience as an object lesson, inviting followers to be fitted for life.

There is truth in both of these explanations of "take my yoke upon you." Both imply the concept of learning, which is part of Jesus' invitation. But I believe that Jesus was being much more simple and direct. He was inviting people to enter into his work. It's generally much easier to work with someone than to work alone.

Many of us have spent our lives plowing our own furrows for Jesus. Yokes were made for two. It is doubly hard to pull a plow and, at the same time, to hold up the dangling side of an empty yoke. What Jesus wants is for us to yoke ourselves up with him and plow his furrow. It is so much easier to plow with him than to plow alone. Jesus doesn't want us to do his work for him. He wants to do his work through us.

Missionary Bob Wakefield of Malaysia expresses this idea in his interpretation of the feeding of the 5,000. The little boy who gave Jesus the five loaves and three fishes must have watched everything closely. When Jesus began to break up the bread and fish, the child probably punched the boy next to him and said proudly, "That's my fish. That's my bread, too." But after several baskets had been filled, he had to admit, "That's not my bread. That's not my fish."

Our bread and fish aren't sufficient to feed the multitudes. Our talents and energy aren't sufficient to do the work of the Lord. When we give them away, count them as ours no more, recognize them as insufficient and insignificant, Jesus multiplies them. Then through us he does what he alone can do.

3. Jesus invites us to learn from him. Let me illustrate. In the quarter-horse country of Texas, ranchers have a unique way of

breaking a two-year-old colt to lead. They halter him up on a long rope with a Spanish burro and turn them loose for a few days in a field. The young horse is so headstrong and energetic that he nearly breaks his neck and heart before he learns to respect his yokefellow on the other end of the rope. When the rancher returns in a few days to untie the donkey, he is able to lead the colt right out of the field. There is much to learn about life at its best when we are yoked with Jesus. Only as we become his yokefellow can we really, in the deepest sense, learn from him.

What happens when we accept the invitation?

We find rest when we accept Jesus' invitation. And, I would add, we find much more effectiveness. Two can do more together than two separately. Becoming a yokefellow of Jesus Christ is like being hooked to a plow with the most powerful tractor that Caterpillar makes. We achieve more in a day with him than in years alone.

And we achieve it without exhaustion, without being heavy laden. This is true for at least two reasons:

1. "My yoke," Jesus says, "fits well." It is an easy yoke to wear. There were no patented yokes in the centuries when oxen were the chief agricultural power. The oxen were driven to the yoke maker and fitted for the yoke. After he had fashioned it, they were brought back and it was tried on. Then other adjustments were made. It was essential that the yoke fit well.

The great thing about taking on the yoke of Jesus is that his always fits us well. It is a yoke made just for me. When we become his yokefellows, we find ourselves doing just what God fashioned and destined us for before we were born.

This is the significance of the gifts of the Spirit in the church. Each person has his or her own yoke. Each is designed to make a unique contribution to the cause of Christ. How much different our churches would be if we allowed people to exercise their gifts. It is in exercising our spiritual gifts that we discover how well the yoke of Jesus fits.

2. We also find rest because the burden of Jesus is light. How does a burden

become light? A burden becomes light when it is something we want to do.

A world-famous preacher tells how as a boy he was sent to pick a quart of berries. He was unhappy about the assignment. On the way to the berry patch, the thought came to him, "What a big surprise it would be for my mother if I picked two quarts!" He hurried to the patch, and in no time, under the excitement of this new motivation, he picked two quarts and enjoyed it. *Why* we do something is important. If we act out of love and our motivation is right, there is no burden.

The old story of the ten-year-old carrying a six-year-old crippled boy on his back is the classic illustration. "That's a mighty heavy burden you've got there, young man," a passerby remarked. "That's no burden," the boy answered. "He's my brother."

The secret of rest is to come to Jesus, to cease from labor in our own strength, and to become a yokefellow in his work. Then we find that his yoke fits us and his work becomes our delight and pleasure. It is a light burden.

CHAPTER FOUR

TAKE OUT THE STOPS

D. L. Moody said there are three kinds of Christians in the world. The first are "third chapter of John" Christians. They have experienced a spiritual rebirth. They have been born, not only of the flesh, but also of the Holy Spirit. The Christian life must begin with a new birth. But it is a tragedy when Christians never go beyond the experience of regeneration.

Second, there are "fourth chapter of John" Christians. They have gone further in the Christian life. Jesus said to the woman of Sychar, speaking of the water in the ancient well of Jacob, "Everyone who drinks of this water will thirst again, but whoever drinks of the water that I shall give him will never thirst; the water that I shall give him will become in him a spring of water, welling up to eternal life" (John 4:13, 14). Such Christians have found that Jesus satisfies. They never thirst. A spring of water wells up in them to eternal life.

Finally, there are "seventh chapter of John" Christians. Jesus was at Jerusalem for one of the great religious feasts. On the last day of the feast in the Temple courtyard, gathered with thousands of other worshipers, Jesus mounted one of the stone curbs and suddenly shouted, "If anyone thirst, let him come to me and drink. He who believes in me, as the scripture has said, 'Out of his heart shall flow rivers of living water' " (John 7:37, 38). It is possible for the Christian to live at a level of life where not only is there a spring in him welling up to eternal life, but there is a river of living water flowing out to others.

Most of us wish that we might become "seventh chapter of John" Christians. John goes on to tell the secret of the river of living water. "Now this he said about the

Spirit, which those who believed in him were to receive; for as yet the Spirit had not been given, because Jesus was not yet glorified." The secret of the river of living water, the secret of living life at its best and for others, is the Holy Spirit. Now, Jesus *has* been glorified. Now, the Holy Spirit *has* been poured out. The Spirit of God who once was only *with* the disciples of Christ now lives *within* them.

This chapter is about the Spirit-filled life. Its object is to outline the way in which the Spirit of God can become a river of living water in your life. However, since the modern Pentecostal movement was born on January 1, 1901, many American Christians have been afraid to delve into the Bible doctrine of the Spirit's fullness. Or they have done so only in reaction to certain manifestations of the Spirit's work that were unacceptable to some segments of the church. It is necessary to spend time on some basic facts about this aspect of Christian life.

Who is the Holy Spirit?

The Holy Spirit is the third person of the triune God. He is truly God. I cannot adequately explain or rationally prove the concept of the Trinity. The Bible nowhere attempts to do so. Neither does the Bible attempt to prove the existence of God. God's existence is assumed. Genesis 1 begins, "In the beginning God." His existence is assumed and affirmed. That is also true of the concept of three personal manifestations of the true God. The Bible speaks of Father, Son, and Holy Spirit. It assigns the properties of deity to all three, discusses the work of each, but affirms that all are really one God.

In the earliest chapters of Genesis and at various times in the Old Testament a certain plurality of the one true God is affirmed (Gen. 1:26; 3:22; Isa. 6:8). In the New Testament a trinity of divine persons is alleged over and over. In Luke 3:22, for example, the Holy Spirit descended on Jesus, who was identified as the Son of God by the voice of the Father. In Matthew 28:19, 20, Christians are commanded to baptize in the name of the Father, Son, and Holy Spirit. Acts 10:36-38 describes Jesus as "Lord of all." Yet it says he was sent by the Father and anointed with the Holy Spirit. In 2 Corinthians 13:14, Paul prays that the grace of Jesus Christ, the love of God, and the fellowship of the Holy Spirit would be with all the Corinthian Christians. (See also John 14:16; Rom. 1:3, 4; 1 Cor. 12:4-6; 2 Cor. 1:21, 22; Titus 3:4-6; Heb. 9:14; 1 Pet. 1:12 and 3:18). Again and again the New Testament assigns personality and divinity to the Holy Spirit.

The Holy Spirit is God. He is not just a divine influence, some shadowy mist from the great unknown, or some other thing that affects humans in some way. Love, joy, and intellect, all properties of a real person, are ascribed to the Holy Spirit. He is God, truly a person, truly divine.

When did the Holy Spirit begin his work?

The Holy Spirit has always been. There was never a time when he was not. His work as we know of it begins with the creation:

> The earth was without form and void, and darkness was upon the face of the deep; and the Spirit of God was moving over the face of the waters (Gen. 1:2).

In the book of Judges, Deborah and the men of God who judged Israel were victorious over their enemies because the Spirit of God possessed them. The prophets of the Old Testament spoke as they were moved by the Holy Spirit. It was the Holy Spirit who overshadowed Mary as the instrument of conception. Jesus Christ, born of a virgin, was begotten by the Holy Spirit. The mighty works of Jesus were done not in his role as the divine Son of God, but as he was filled and empowered by the Holy Spirit. The life and ministry of Jesus was, therefore, the product of the Holy Spirit's work (Luke 4:14).

But something new happened on the day of Pentecost. John the Baptist had prophesied that Jesus would baptize with the Holy Spirit and with fire (Matt. 3:11). On the day of his ascension, Jesus promised his church that they would be baptized with the Holy Spirit "before many days had passed." They were to wait for the "promise of the Father" about which he had previously told them (Acts 1:4, 5). This referred to the "Comforter like Jesus" promised in John 14:16, 17. The coming of the Comforter was dependent on Jesus' return to the Father. Jesus had promised that the Spirit of truth would come and would never leave them. This Spirit, he told them, already was with them but would be in them.

That promise was kept on the day of Pentecost. The Holy Spirit was poured out on the church. He moved into the church as a whole and filled each individual. The age of the Holy Spirit had dawned.

Why was the Holy Spirit given?

Many answers could be given to this question. In John 14—17, Jesus described many aspects of the Holy Spirit's ministry. All of these, however, can be reduced to one common denominator: The Holy Spirit was given to make known and to magnify Jesus Christ.

> He will glorify me, for he will take what is mine and declare it to you (John 16:14).

Jesus Christ came to make known the Father (John 14:5-10). The Holy Spirit was given to glorify and make known the Son.

This might be illustrated in several ways.

The Holy Spirit was given to make the presence of Jesus universal. The ascension of Jesus was a distinct advantage for the church. His return to the Father made the coming of the Holy Spirit possible. He was the ascension-gift of the risen and glorified Christ. Christ was limited by his incarnation. His humanity confined him in time and space. By the ministry of the Holy Spirit, Jesus' presence could become universal:

> Nevertheless I tell you the truth: it is to your advantage that I go away, for if I do not go away, the Counselor will not come to you; but if I go, I will send him to you. And when he comes, he will convince the world of sin and of righteousness and of judgment: of sin, because they do not believe in me; of righteousness, because I go to the Father, and you will see me no more; of judgment, because the ruler of this world is judged (John 16:7-11).

The Holy Spirit was given to make the person of Jesus known to all people. It is the Holy Spirit who reveals Jesus to us. It is the Holy Spirit who makes Jesus a reality in the Christian's life. The ministry of the

Holy Spirit is to glorify Jesus and make his righteousness and power known to us.

So, when a person is filled with the Holy Spirit, he is filled with Christ. When a person is controlled by the Holy Spirit, he is controlled by Christ. The Holy Spirit has one primary task: to magnify and make known Jesus Christ.

What is the Holy Spirit's ministry in the life of a Christian?

The New Testament describes at least six ministries of the Holy Spirit:

1. The Holy Spirit regenerates the Christian. It was Nicodemus, a moral, cultured, religious leader of first-century Judaism, to whom Jesus stressed the necessity of a new birth. "Unless one is born of water and the Spirit, he cannot enter the kingdom of God" (John 3:5). Salvation is only "by the washing of regeneration and renewal in the Holy Spirit" (Titus 3:5).

No matter who you are, how good you are, how much you know, or how religious you may be by natural inclination, you become a Christian only through a new birth wrought by the ministry of the Holy Spirit.

2. The Holy Spirit indwells the Christian. When you become a Christian, the Holy Spirit makes his home in you. "Do you not know that your body is a temple of the Holy Spirit within you, which you have from God?" (1 Cor. 6:19).

The moment you become a Christian, the Holy Spirit takes up his abode in your heart. This is what Peter referred to on the day of Pentecost when he was asked, "What shall we do?" He replied, "Repent, and be baptized every one of you in the name of Jesus Christ for the forgiveness of your sins; and you shall receive the gift of the Holy Spirit" (Acts 2:38). When you become a Christian, you receive the gift which is the Holy Spirit. He indwells you.

This means, then, that the fullness of the Holy Spirit in the Christian's life is not something else coming in from outside. It is not a second, additional something or someone that the Christian receives after the new birth. When you have Christ you have everything (Col. 2:9). The fullness of the Holy Spirit means to permit him who already lives in you to fill your entire life.

3. The Holy Spirit seals the Christian. "In him you also, who have heard the word of truth, the gospel of your salvation, and have believed in him, were sealed with the promised Holy Spirit" (Eph. 1:13).

What does this mean? The word *seal* originally referred to a few drops of hot wax used to seal a letter or document. Then the person who sealed the document would put his own personal mark in that hot wax. It was the mark of a particular individual. We seldom use this method of sealing today.

In some parts of the American west, ranchers still brand their cattle. If they produce some registered breed of livestock for market, almost without exception each beast receives an indelible tattoo in its ear. It has the mark of its breeder and owner. With this indelible mark it is identified or sealed.

This is a ministry that the Holy Spirit performs in the Christian. He is the mark, the seal, that sets us apart as belonging to God. He brands us as the children of God until the day of ultimate redemption.

4. The Holy Spirit is the guarantee of the Christian's eternal inheritance "until we acquire possession of it, to the praise of his

glory" (Eph. 1:14). Paul told the Corinthian Christians, "It is God who establishes us with you in Christ, and has commissioned us; he has put his seal upon us and given us his Spirit in our hearts as a guarantee" (2 Cor. 1:22).

What does this mean? The old word for guarantee is "earnest." It means down payment, a promise of what is to come. When you purchase a house or other real estate it is common to make an offer and attach to it a sum called "earnest money." That earnest money, if the terms of the offer are otherwise met, is your guarantee to go through with your part of the agreement.

The Holy Spirit has a comparable ministry in your life. He is the guarantee of what is to come when God has finished his work in us. He is a foretaste of heaven on the way to heaven. If you are not experiencing a little bliss on the way to heaven, you are missing what God has intended. The joy, peace, and power of the Holy Spirit in your life is a preview of what the Father has planned for his children.

5. The Holy Spirit is the element in which one is immersed into the body of Christ. John the Baptist promised that one was coming after him who would baptize *in*

the Holy Spirit just as he baptized *in* water
(Matt. 3:11; Mark 1:18; Luke 3:16; John
1:33). John pointed to Jesus as the Lamb of
God, God's anointed and unique Son, whose
coming John was sent to announce (John
1:29-34). Just before his ascension, Jesus
reminded his disciples that "John baptized
with water," but that in a few days they would
be "baptized with the Holy Spirit" (Acts
1:5). (The Greek word translated "with" is
en. It means "with" or "in.") The Holy
Spirit is not the baptizer. The Holy Spirit is
the element in which or the instrument by
which the baptism takes place.

The same Greek word is used in
1 Corinthians 12:13. It should read, "For *in*
(or *with;* not *by*) one Spirit we were all
baptized into one body—Jews or Greeks,
slaves or free—and all were made to drink
of one Spirit." By being immersed in the
Holy Spirit, we become a part of Christ's
body, the church. "Do you not know
that your bodies are members of Christ?"
(1 Cor. 6:15). Whether black or white, male
or female, young or old, all Christians are
members of Christ's body. It is in the Holy
Spirit that the body of Christ is one body,
though made up of many members (1 Cor.
12:28). It is he who gives each member of

Christ's body his own gift "for the common good" (1 Cor. 12:7). The Holy Spirit enables us to be gifted members of the body of Christ.

6. The Holy Spirit fills the Christian for holy living and effective service. There is a difference, however, in this ministry of the Holy Spirit in the Christian's life and the other five. The Christian is regenerated only once. The Holy Spirit comes to dwell in the Christian forever (John 14:16). The Holy Spirit seals the Christian only once and that sealing lasts until the day of redemption. The Holy Spirit is the once-for-all guarantee of the Christian's inheritance in God. If the guarantee can be withdrawn, it is no guarantee. When you receive Christ, you become a member of the body of Christ. All of these things happen only once, and once for all.

When you study the Spirit's "filling" ministry in the Bible, you find that it happens over and over again. You are not filled once for all. Read the early chapters of Acts. You will find that though the Christians were filled on the day of Pentecost, they were also filled on other occasions. In fact, the fullness of the Holy

Spirit in the Christian's life is to be
appropriated every day.

This is a fundamental concept that most
evangelical Christians have difficulty
grasping. We have long labored under the
illusion that sometime, if you were lucky,
or very devout, or extra prayerful, you
might be filled with the Holy Spirit. The
opposite is true. Every new Christian is filled
with the Holy Spirit when he is saved. We
have greatly sinned against new Christians
because we have not told them how to stay
filled, or how to appropriate the fullness
every day.

What does the filling of the Spirit mean?
Years ago, Ruth Paxson underscored three
things the Holy Spirit does when he fills a
Christian.

First, when the Holy Spirit fills we realize
the presence of Jesus in our lives.
Multitudes of Christians live as if they were
completely alone in the world. They live
only by "feeling." (When they feel good,
Christ is with them. When they are low or
discouraged, they are alone.) The truth is that
Jesus Christ is with us and in us, in the
person of the Holy Spirit, whether we feel
like it or not. When we allow the Holy
Spirit to fill our lives we begin to live in the

light of that fact rather than in the wake of fluctuating feelings. No mood or circumstance drives Jesus out of our life. He is with us. That realization should make us men and women of courage and confidence.

Second, when the Holy Spirit fills us he recreates the holy life of Jesus in us. He does something far better than to help us do something difficult. What he wants to do is relive his holy life in us.

> But we have this treasure in earthen vessels, to show that the transcendent power belongs to God and not to us. We are afflicted in every way, but not crushed; perplexed, but not driven to despair; persecuted, but not forsaken; struck down, but not destroyed; always carrying in the body the death of Jesus, so that the life of Jesus may also be manifested in our bodies. For while we live we are always being given up to death for Jesus' sake, so that the life of Jesus may be manifested in our mortal flesh (2 Cor. 4:7-11).

The Holy Spirit, when he fills your life, manifests the life of Jesus in your own body. He wants your hands to be his hands, your feet his feet, your mind his mind, and your heart his heart. Galatians 2:20 says it all:

> I have been crucified with Christ; it is no longer I who live, but Christ who lives in me; and the life I now live in the flesh I live by faith in the Son of God who loved me and gave himself for me.

Third, when the Holy Spirit fills you, he reproduces the mighty works of Jesus in your life. So few Christians lead lives of victory. So few know the rivers of living water that flow out to others. Yet this is God's intention for every Christian. It is not his intention that Christians exert great influence by dint of their own personality, talents, or public relations skills. It is his intention that every Christian lead a life of supernatural victory in which Jesus would again, himself, through the Holy Spirit, perform his mighty works. "Thanks be to God," Paul said, "who in Christ always leads us in triumph, and through us spreads the fragrance of the knowledge of him everywhere" (2 Cor. 2:14).

That verse has actually come true in my life in the past few years in ways that overwhelm me. After fifteen years of reasonably successful pastorates, which God had surely blessed, a series of events led me to reevaluate my ministry. To my dismay I discovered that it was based primarily on three things: hard work, doing a fair job in the pulpit, and, when I really needed it, my ability to turn on the charm.

I began to be honest and open about what I was and what I did. I confessed my sins, made apology and restitution where necessary, and experienced the joy and direct fellowship with God that follows his cleansing. I thought that perhaps I might be experiencing the fullness of the Holy Spirit in my life, but I didn't openly claim it because of fear others might think I was either bragging or had gone berserk. I didn't know how to tell anyone else how to be filled.

The church I served as pastor sent me to Detroit for a conference. In that conference, what I had hoped might possibly be true was confirmed. I returned home saying, "I have been filled with the Holy Spirit, and I can tell you how you can be filled."

The way God has made me a "fragrance of the knowledge of him everywhere" since then is amazing. Every week for several months, and almost every week during these past years, God has led someone into my life who is just ready to find Christ. I have led more people personally to Christ just by accident than I did before on purpose.

I insist that this can be only the Holy Spirit reproducing the mighty power of Jesus in my life.

How can you be filled with the Holy Spirit?

There are three prerequisites for you to be filled with the Holy Spirit.

The first is *honesty*. Are you honest before God and man about what you are and what you do? Have you truthfully taken off the mask? Have you exposed yourself to the light of God, confessed your sins to God, and accepted with joy the work of Jesus Christ your advocate?

Have you been honest about your self? Have you taken up the cross? Have you counted yourself as dead with Christ, and buried, and now risen with him?

The Holy Spirit does not fill dirty vessels. You have no power to cleanse your life or win the victory over self. But Jesus Christ has. If you will agree with him about what you do and what you are, he will cleanse you. He already knows what you do and are. Confession is not telling him what he doesn't know but agreeing with him about the sinfulness in your life.

The second prerequisite is *hunger*. Do you want to continue as you are? Do you want to spend your life in the third chapter of John? If you're satisfied with life as it is, you will never know life at its best. "Blessed are those," Jesus said, "who hunger and thirst after righteousness, for they shall be satisfied" (Matt. 5:6). If you don't hunger for the Holy Spirit to fill all your life, to produce in you the life and work of Jesus, it will never happen. If you don't want him to reign in your life, and be Lord of all you are and do, you will never be filled with the Spirit.

The third prerequisite to the Spirit-filled life is simply *appropriating his fullness by faith.* You are filled with the Spirit in the same way that you are born of the Spirit, through faith. The Holy Spirit's fullness is not the reward of much prayer, long years of sacrificial and obedient living, or the result of esoteric knowledge. "Did you receive the Spirit by works of the law, or by hearing with faith? . . . Does he who supplies the Spirit to you and works miracles among you do so by works of the law, or by hearing with faith?" (Gal. 3:2-5).

It is strange that devout Christians, who have been so faithful to insist that we are not made right with God by deeds of law and flesh, would nevertheless spend hour upon hour, year upon year, trying to be good enough to be filled with the Holy Spirit. The Lord has commanded us, "Be filled with the Spirit" (Eph. 5:18). But try as we will, we cannot fill ourselves. Christ has promised that if we ask anything according to the will of God, he will do it. Ask him to fill you with his Spirit, and then take him at his word that he has.

Don't expect something from without to come in. Being filled with the Holy Spirit isn't like pumping up a rubber life raft with a hand pump. It is, rather, like opening the valve on a bottle of compressed air that is already in the life raft. The Holy Spirit already dwells in you. By faith, take out the stops that keep him closed away in some corner of your life and let him fill you with himself.

Keys to exercising faith

1. Let me reemphasize the necessity for real honesty about your *self*. If you still harbor the thought that you can be a blessing to the cause of Christ, if you haven't come to the end of yourself, with all your talents, skills, personality, and dedication, you haven't seen the truth about your self. The only hope you have is "Christ in you." The glory of a peach seed is the tree it can become. Its hope of glory is the germ of life within. Hope can become reality only when the seed gives up its natural character to death. As long as you cling to your self, even your best self, you will never become what God intended you to be.

2. Ask God to fill you with his Spirit. Be specific. Don't say, "I want you to fill me." Or, "Help me to be filled." Say, "Lord, I need to be filled. I cannot fill myself, so fill me with your Spirit now." For years I prayed, "Lord, I want to surrender to you. Help me to do it." What a new day when I

began to say, "Lord, I surrender." To be sure, I knew that some things might arise that I wouldn't wish to surrender. But I trusted those things to him too. Ask God to fill and control your life with his Holy Spirit.

3. Now thank him. The will of God is for us to be filled with the Spirit. The willingness of the Father cannot be disputed. "If you then, who are evil, know how to give good gifts to your children, how much more will the heavenly Father give the Holy Spirit to those who ask him?" (Luke 11:13). The promise of God is sure. "This is the confidence which we have in him that if we ask anything according to his will he hears us. And if we know that he hears us in whatever we ask, we know that we have obtained the requests made of him" (1 John 5:14, 15).

Take him at his word. Don't despair if you don't experience a certain feeling. Feeling follows the fact. God will give you the feeling in his time. Don't wait on some special sign or gift. Cling to God's Word. Thank God for filling every part of your life with his indwelling Spirit and expect that Spirit to manifest his fullness in your life.